The HOPE of EASTER

OUTREACH

The Hope of Easter

Published by Outreach, Inc. Colorado Springs, CO 80919
www.Outreach.com

ISBN: 9781942027355

Cover Design and Interior Design by Tim Downs

Written by Joshua Cooley

Edited by Darla Hightower

Printed in the United States of America

CONTENTS

INTRODUCTION

Hope is a beautiful word.

To hope is to look forward to a specific outcome, to wish for a particular ending, to dream about a goal. Hope is a common pastime in our lives. We often hope for good health, a better-paying job, a bigger house, a car that doesn't leak oil, more kids (or less!), better political candidates, reconciliation in broken relationships, a shorter commute, a longer vacation, world peace, healing for a sick loved one, fewer bills, more athletic skills, and for relatives who don't act like they're from Mars.

There are other, more sobering types of hope. The frightened parents sitting bedside in the pediatric unit hope their little boy will be cured of cancer. The weary refugee from a war-torn country hopes to find a better life. The gaunt urchin in a developing nation hopes to find food for the day.

Hope is a powerful force. It encourages us, motivates us, gives us purpose, and even impacts the course of our lives. But hopes aren't always realized. They are often dashed against the harsh realities of life, like a storm-tossed ship crashing into jagged rocks. Hope that is lost is one of life's greatest tragedies.

There is, however, another type of hope that never disappoints. In Scripture, the word **hope** means more than just mere desire. It's different from **want**, **wish**, or **need**. It transcends raw craving or a longing that might go unfulfilled.

Biblically defined, **hope** means "to expect with confidence." Christian hope, in other words, is the eager anticipation of a guaranteed outcome. This is the hope of Easter.

The hope of Easter is found in the gospel message—the good news that a holy God has freely offered love, forgiveness, reconciliation, and eternal life to sinful humanity. The hope of Easter provides unique, lasting joy and peace. And it all has to do with a world-changing event that took place two thousand years ago in a small garden just outside the walls of ancient Jerusalem.

On that Sunday morning in the first century, several Jewish women awoke while it was still dark to visit a sepulcher. Their mission? To anoint a three-day-old corpse with spices and ointments, part of a Jewish burial ritual that had been interrupted by the timing of the death, which occurred shortly before the advent of the Sabbath the preceding Friday afternoon.

The dead man was Jesus of Nazareth. His death had crushed many dreams. Throughout Palestine, people had hoped that He was the long-awaited Messiah, God's promised Redeemer. But at the height of Passover, the Jewish holy week, a bloodthirsty mob called for His execution and the Romans consented, crucifying the sinless Son of God between two criminals.

When the women arrived at the tomb that morning, though, they found it empty—the greatest news in history! Jesus wasn't dead anymore. He had come back to life!

Jesus' resurrection changed everything. It was the climax of God's great plan of salvation for mankind, providing hope to lost sinners. God's Son miraculously incarnated to earth to live a perfect life, suffer a sacrificial death, resurrect in glorious power, and provide eternal salvation to all who trust in Him. The resurrection provides hope of new life—innumerable spiritual blessings in this life and the life to come. The resurrection guarantees that our hope isn't in vain. It's heaven's authenticating seal of approval.

No matter where you are in your spiritual journey, the goal of this book remains the same: to proclaim Scripture's truth about the death and resurrection of Jesus so that you might marvel—either anew or for the very first time—at God's love, mercy, and forgiveness through Christ.

This is the hope of Easter. Those who believe are changed forever.

CHAPTER 1

THE HISTORY

The legions are storming the gates.

Each Easter, armies of pastel-clad parishioners, dressed in their Sunday finest, flock to churches throughout the United States. Attendance figures swell to totals that most places of worship won't experience again for another 365 days. In 2015, half of all Americans said they planned to attend an Easter service, according to a CNN report.[1]

Easter's popularity, though, extends far beyond stained-glass windows. Each spring, the confection industry launches an all-out sugar assault on the public. Their weapons of choice? Chocolate bunnies, jelly beans, marshmallow chicks, caramel-filled eggs, and all manner of other teeth-rotting delights. Americans spend more than $2 billion annually on Easter candy.[2]

Yes, Easter is a big deal. Like Christmas, it's a unique and somewhat bizarre intermingling of the sacred and secular. So how did we get **here**? To understand the hope of Easter, we first need to ask: Why do we celebrate Easter?

Ironically, for all the hubbub surrounding Easter, its true origins remain a mystery. The term **Easter**, of course, is not found anywhere in the Bible. No one knows for sure when people started observing the holiday, although some evidence points to the second century.

This much we do know: the English word **Easter** traces its lineage back to the Greek word **Pascha**, which is derived from the Hebrew term **pesach**, meaning "Passover." For more than three thousand years, the Passover has been one of the most important observances on the Jewish calendar, commanded by God Himself in Exodus 12 as an annual celebration of Israel's deliverance from Egyptian slavery.

The first Passover coincided with the last of the ten plagues—the death of every firstborn male in Egypt—that God inflicted upon Israel's captors to free His people. For Israel to avoid this terrible judgment, God required a blood sacrifice. He commanded every Israelite family to slaughter an unblemished one-year-old male lamb and sprinkle its blood on the doorposts on their house. Later that night, as God brought justice upon Egypt, He saw the lamb's blood on each Hebrew dwelling and withheld judgment, **passing over** those houses in mercy.

As Exodus 12:12–13 says:

> *On that same night I will pass through Egypt and strike down every firstborn of both people and animals, and I will bring judgment on all the gods of Egypt. I am the LORD. The blood will be a sign for you on the houses where you are, and when I see the blood, I will pass over you. No destructive plague will touch you when I strike Egypt.*

Why did God call for Israel to perform this unique ritual? Why couldn't He have just spared the Jews without the slaughter of thousands of lambs? Ultimately, the ceremony foreshadowed God's Son, Jesus Christ, and His sacrifice on the cross for the sins of mankind.

Both the Old and New Testaments make it quite clear that Christ was the true **Paschal Lamb**, the perfect fulfillment of the Old Testament sacrificial system that God gave His people on Mount Sinai. Here are several examples:

- Referring to Jesus in his famous "Suffering Servant" prophecy, Isaiah wrote, "Like a lamb that is led to the slaughter, and like a sheep that before its shearers is silent, so he opened not his mouth." (Isaiah 53:7, ESV)
- "The next day John [the Baptist] saw Jesus coming toward him and said, 'Look, the Lamb of God, who takes away the sin of the world!'" (John 1:29)
- "For Christ, our Passover lamb, has been sacrificed." (1 Corinthians 5:7)
- "You were ransomed from the futile ways inherited from your forefathers, not with perishable things such as silver or gold, but with the precious blood of Christ, like that of a lamb without blemish or spot." (1 Peter 1:18–19, ESV)

That the Messiah was crucified during Passover week (John 19:14) was no accident. Jesus was making a powerfully tacit statement in revealing Himself as the perfect fulfillment of Old Testament Law—a point the apostles did not miss in their New Testament writings.

After the early church started, following the Day of Pentecost (Acts 2), the first Christians (literally, "Christ followers") started gathering together for weekly worship services on Sundays, or "the Lord's Day" (Revelation 1:10), to honor the day on which the resurrection occurred. Eventually, believers started commemorating Christ's triumph over death with an annual festival we now call Easter.

These days, most churches in the western hemisphere celebrate Easter anywhere between March 22 and April 25, while Eastern Orthodox churches usually observe it a week or two later. Over the centuries, a wide variety of Easter traditions—some solemn, many strange—have sprung up. In Sweden, girls dress up like witches and go trick-or-treating. In Bermuda, people fly kites on Good Friday to signify Jesus' ascension. And in Venezuela and Greece, people burn effigies of Judas Iscariot.[3]

In the United States, Hallmark cards, honey-glazed hams, egg hunts, and rabbit-head PEZ dispensers have infiltrated the festivities. Some Christians wring their hands at all this good, old-fashioned American commercialization. Others embrace it.

Either way, let's not miss the point. For true followers of Christ, what's most important about Easter is not its origins, traditions, or even the very institution itself, but rather the glorious truth that it celebrates. The Son of God is alive, and His victory over death provides eternal, life-changing hope!

1 Amy Roberts, "Easter by the Numbers," *CNN Library*, updated April 2, 2015, http://www.cnn.com/2013/03/29/living/easter-by-the-numbers/.

2 Lauren Torissi, "90 Million Chocolate Bunnies and Other Fun Easter Facts," *Good Morning America*, April 6, 2012, http://abcnews.go.com/blogs/lifestyle/2012/04/90-million-chocolate-bunnies-and-other-fun-easter-facts/.

3 "Easter," History.com, 2009, http://www.history.com/topics/holidays/history-of-easter.

CHAPTER 2

THE NEED FOR SALVATION

Why do we need hope?

Sure, life has its challenges—some of them quite significant—but all in all, things often have a way of working themselves out, right? So what's the big deal? Are we in some sort of imminent danger from an alien invasion, perhaps? Or an army of zombies? A modern-day bubonic plague? A giant meteor hurtling toward earth? Higher taxes? Another **Rocky** movie?

The hope of Easter addresses a completely different problem. To understand this hope—and why we desperately need it—we must go back to the very beginning. To paradise.

"In the beginning," Genesis 1:1 says, "God created the heavens and the earth." This is where the hope of Easter starts. If we fail to accept the truth of divine creation, everything else is meaningless.

The universe was not a random explosion of microscopic particles that somehow evolved over billions of years into the ordered cosmos we marvel at today. Our ancestors were **not** infinitesimal organisms that somehow survived a raging primordial soup. The universe and everything in it, including humans, came from a loving, personal Creator. As Psalm 139:13–14 says, "For you created my inmost being; you knit me together in my mother's womb. I praise you because I am fearfully and wonderfully made."

When God spoke the universe into existence, it was perfect. Because He is holy, omniscient, and all-powerful, God cannot make anything evil or blemished. All of creation flawlessly reflected His glory. After each of the six days of creation, God surveyed what He had miraculously wrought and "saw that it was good" (Genesis 1:10).

This perfection extended to the first man and woman, the magnum opus of God's breathtaking handiwork. He made humans to fellowship with Him, worship Him, and spread His glory in His vast universe. But God didn't want to interact with mere robots—mindless automatons whose obedience was strictly the result of initial hardwiring. So in His divine wisdom and sovereignty, He created flesh-and-blood creatures in His own image (Genesis 1:27). He gave minds, hearts, and free wills to His image-bearers so they could choose to love and obey their Creator of their own volition and fully enter into worship.

God dearly loved Adam and Eve. He blessed them with every delight and enjoyed intimate fellowship with them, even condescending to walk and speak with them among the Garden of Eden's beauty (Genesis 3:8).

But Adam and Eve made a disastrous choice. They chose to reject their Creator's loving rule over them. Deceived by Satan, God's ancient adversary who was disguised as a crafty serpent, they arrogantly ate some fruit from the Tree of the Knowledge of Good and Evil, which God had expressly forbidden. As Genesis 3:6 says, "When the woman saw that the fruit of the tree was good for food and pleasing to the eye, and also desirable for gaining wisdom, she took some and ate it. She also gave some to her husband, who was with her, and he ate it."

Adam and Eve's willful rejection of God's command ushered sin into the world. Like a devastating pestilence, sin marred God's perfect creation and caused a cataclysmic rift between the Creator and the created. Sadness, shame, pain, sickness, hate, and—worst of all—death became realities. God cast Adam and Eve out of Eden. Paradise—perfect, intimate fellowship between the heavenly Father and His children—was lost.

The aftermath of sin didn't end with Adam and Eve, though. Sin's curse has extended to every human being in history. The whole world, in fact, is accountable to God (Romans 3:19).

As Adam's seed, we all have inherited a sinful nature and stand guilty before God from the time we are born. Put it this way: When it comes to human culpability, there is no Switzerland. Neutral ground doesn't exist. As Romans 5:18 says, "One trespass resulted in condemnation for all people." Many other Scripture references affirm this, including these:

- "Surely I was sinful at birth, sinful from the time my mother conceived me." (Psalm 51:5)

- "There is no one righteous, not even one; there is no one who understands; there is no one who seeks God." (Romans 3:10–11)
- "For all have sinned and fall short of the glory of God." (Romans 3:23)

Sin's immediate consequences are spiritual alienation from God and ultimately death. Romans 6:23 explains that "the wages of sin is death," and Romans 5:12 says, "So death spread to all men because all sinned" (ESV). Likewise, Ephesians 2:3 says, "Like the rest, we were by nature deserving of wrath."

The Bible clearly states that God's final judgment against unregenerate sinners is eternal separation from Him and punishment in hell. The descriptions of hell in Scripture are frightening:

- "Outer darkness" (Matthew 8:12, ESV)
- A "blazing furnace, where there will be weeping and gnashing of teeth" (Matthew 13:42)
- A place where "the smoke of their torment will rise for ever and ever" and "there will be no rest day or night" (Revelation 14:11)

- A "lake of fire" and "the second death" (Revelation 20:14)

Many people take offense to the notion of hell. How, they ask, can a loving God sentence people to such a terrible fate? But this attitude fails to acknowledge a simple but vital fact: We are the created, not the Creator. God makes the rules. If it weren't for Him, we wouldn't even exist. The apostle Paul addressed this when he wrote in Romans 9:14–24:

> *What then shall we say? Is God unjust? Not at all! For he says to Moses, "I will have mercy on whom I have mercy, and I will have compassion on whom I have compassion."*
>
> *It does not, therefore, depend on human desire or effort, but on God's mercy. For Scripture says to Pharaoh: "I raised you up for this very purpose, that I might display my power in you and that my name might be proclaimed in all the earth." Therefore God has mercy on*

whom he wants to have mercy, and he hardens whom he wants to harden.

One of you will say to me: "Then why does God still blame us? For who is able to resist his will?" But who are you, a human being, to talk back to God? "Shall what is formed say to the one who formed it, 'Why did you make me like this?'" Does not the potter have the right to make out of the same lump of clay some pottery for special purposes and some for common use?

What if God, although choosing to show his wrath and make his power known, bore with great patience the objects of his wrath—prepared for destruction? What if he did this to make the riches of his glory known to the objects of his mercy, whom he prepared in advance for glory—even us, whom he also called, not only from the Jews but also from the Gentiles?

This is a difficult truth. It requires a shift from the prevalent humanistic mind-set to accepting this vital fact: God owes us nothing. As the eternal, all-powerful, omniscient Creator, God possesses divine prerogative over all matters in His creation. It's His world, He makes the rules, and we have to be okay with that.

But the existence of hell and God's wrath against sin isn't just about divine rights. It's also about God's character. Because He is just and holy (perfectly righteous, morally pure, and set apart from anything in creation), God's nature **requires** that sin be punished. Sin is an affront to God's glory and righteousness. To **not** punish sin would violate God's justice and, in fact, His very essence.

As such, God would have fully been within His rights to utterly forsake His creation and abandon us to sin's deadly corruption. But He didn't! That's the beauty of Romans 6:23, mentioned above. It starts with bad news ("For the wages of sin is death . . ."), but ends with this glorious truth: "but the gift of God is eternal life in Christ Jesus our Lord."

There is hope for fallen mankind! God's justice is perfectly balanced with love and grace. Immediately after the Fall, God mercifully intertwined a hint of coming salvation with pronouncements of judgment. During His curse on Satan, God declared, "And I will put enmity between you and the woman, and between your offspring and hers; he will crush your head, and you will strike his heel" (Genesis 3:15). The woman's "offspring" was Jesus. This was a foreshadowing of messianic redemption!

Bear in mind this, too: sin's entrée didn't catch God by surprise. When Adam and Eve rebelled, God didn't hastily convene a heavenly crisis response subcommittee. Human events don't startle or stun God. He never switches to plan B. The Fall was completely within His control because He is sovereign (2 Samuel 7:22), holy (Leviticus 19:2), eternal (Deuteronomy 33:27), all-knowing (1 John 3:20), and all-powerful (Jeremiah 32:17).

God, in fact, put His wondrous plan of salvation in motion in what theologians call "eternity past," that mysterious epoch that predates creation. At the center of God the Father's plan was the incarnation of God the Son. Jesus did not begin in the Bethlehem manger. As the second Person of the triune God, Jesus has always existed. Colossians 1:15 affirms His eternal nature when it says He is "the firstborn over all creation." Likewise, John 1:1 says of Jesus, "In the beginning was the Word, and the Word was with God, and the Word was God." Revelation 1:18 concurs when it says that Jesus is "alive for ever and ever!"

Pause for a moment and reflect on what you've just read. Are you amazed by God's love for you? Are you astounded by the scope of this cosmic rescue mission that exceeds the bounds of time? You should be! But wait. There's more . . .

When God set His salvation plan in motion in eternity past, He didn't stop at anointing His own Son as the vehicle of redemption. He sovereignly selected the recipients of that Christ-fueled grace. As Ephesians 1:4–5 says, "He chose us in him **before** the creation of the world to be holy and blameless in his sight" (emphasis added). Likewise, 2 Timothy 1:9 says that God's "grace was given us in Christ Jesus **before** the beginning of time" (emphasis added). Long before the world began, God predestined many to receive His love and forgiveness (Romans 8:29–30; 2 Thessalonians 2:13; 1 Peter 1:1–2). This, in part, explains why the apostle John was overwhelmed with joyful awe when he exclaimed in 1 John 3:1, “See what great love the Father has lavished on us, that we should be called children of God!”

To convey this marvelous reconciliation plan to mankind, God first selected a man named Abraham, whom He promised to make into a great nation, Israel, and bless all the peoples of earth (Genesis 12:1–3). For centuries, the Lord showered His love on Israel and spoke to His people through godly prophets in the Old Testament. In the New Testament, He used the apostles to speak His truth.

This is how the Bible, God’s Word, came into being. From Genesis to Revelation, the Bible is comprised of sixty-six books written by approximately forty authors over at least thirteen hundred years. But it’s not a random, outdated collection of ancient laws, legends, proverbs, and poetry. It is the inerrant, inspired Word of God, divinely breathed into existence through the pens of human authors to record how heaven’s message of hope has unfolded throughout history.

As 2 Timothy 3:16 states, “All Scripture is God-breathed." Second Peter 1:20–21 puts it this way: "Above all, you must understand that no prophecy of Scripture came about by the prophet's own interpretation of things. For prophecy never had its origin in the human will, but prophets, though human, spoke from God as they were carried along by the Holy Spirit."

The Bible tells a cohesive—and still perfectly relevant—story of hope through the saving work of God's Son. From the earliest pages of the Old Testament, implicit whispers of Jesus—and many explicit shouts—fill the Scriptures. Jesus Himself testified after His resurrection that "Moses and all the Prophets" bore witness to Him (Luke 24:27).

We see allusions to the coming Messiah in the sacrifice of Isaac (Genesis 22; John 1:29), the Passover (Exodus 12), the bronze serpent (Numbers 21:4–9; John 3:14), and the life of Jonah (Matthew 12:38–40), to name a few. Christ appears in hundreds of Old Testament prophecies that provide details on everything from the place of His birth (Micah 5:2) to His crucifixion (Psalm 34:20) to His eternal reign (Daniel 7:12–13). God even used ancient Israel's long history of spiritual unfaithfulness to point ahead to the Messiah in passages such as Isaiah 9, Jeremiah 33, and Ezekiel 37.

Then . . . silence. After Malachi, the final book of the Old Testament, God provided no spoken or written word for more than four hundred years. The Jews waited . . . and waited . . . and waited for the promised Deliverer. In the meantime, the world was changing rapidly. Great empires rose and fell with alarming speed. Yet it seemed like the Lord's redemption would never come.

But hope was on the way.

CHAPTER 3

THE FIRST COMING

When emperors made an entrance in ancient times, they were often accompanied by great fanfare. Flanked by a large entourage, the ruler would parade through the streets as his royal chariot cut a swath through the teeming throng. The king wanted to see and be seen. He wanted all his power, glory, and opulence on display.

But not **this** King.

On that blessed night in Bethlehem more than two thousand years ago, the eternal King of kings and Lord of lords quietly came to earth—the one He created—as a helpless baby boy. A heavenly choir of angels announced His birth to some shocked shepherds on the outskirts of town, and later, a small group of Near Eastern stargazers came to pay homage. Otherwise, this miraculous moment went largely unnoticed.

His royal bedroom was a dirty farm stable. His bed was a rough wooden manger. And the witnesses to His birth? Smelly livestock.

Jesus' great mission of hope humbly started in the unlikeliest of places . . . and in the most unlikely of ways. The incarnation—God the Son becoming flesh and condescending to earth as fully God and fully man—is history's greatest miracle. Its truth stretches the limits of human comprehension and still produces astonishment and wonder. The hope of Easter wouldn't have been possible without the reality of Bethlehem.

Consider the awe-filled words of Paul in Philippians 2:5–7: "Christ Jesus: Who, being in very nature God, did not consider equality with God something to be used to his own advantage; rather, he made himself nothing by taking the very nature of a servant, being made in human likeness." Similarly, John marveled when he started his gospel by connecting the dots between Christ's preincarnate and incarnate states:

- "In the beginning was the Word, and the Word was with God, and the Word was God. He was with God in the beginning. Through him all things were made; without him nothing was made that has been made." (John 1:1–3)
- "The Word became flesh and made his dwelling

among us. We have seen his glory, the glory of the one and only Son, who came from the Father, full of grace and truth." (John 1:14)

Jesus' true nature and purpose remained largely concealed until He was about thirty years old (Luke 3:23). At that point, He began His public ministry, proclaiming the glorious gospel of salvation to the people of Palestine and performing incredible miracles to validate His messianic claims. "The time has come," He told the multitudes. "The kingdom of God has come near. Repent and believe the good news!" (Mark 1:15).

Sadly, few did. Jesus' message of hope largely fell on deaf ears during His time on earth. For three years, massive crowds followed Him, enraptured by His unique teachings and miraculous works. But not many actually came to saving faith. The general public was expecting a political and military-minded Messiah, one who would free Israel from Roman rule. The corrupt, Jewish, religious establishment viewed Him as a blasphemous fraud and a threat to their position. Even His own family and disciples struggled initially to understand His true nature and mission. Once, Jesus' mother and brothers tried to break through the crowd and take Jesus home because they thought He had gone off the deep end (Mark 3:21)!

Jesus had come to offer salvation to Israel—God's chosen people, the seed of the great patriarch Abraham—yet they rejected Him. In Matthew 13:14–15, Jesus applied the prophetic words of Isaiah 6 to His first-century listeners:

In them is fulfilled the prophecy of Isaiah:

"You will be ever hearing but never understanding;
you will be ever seeing but never perceiving.

For this people's heart has become calloused;
they hardly hear with their ears,
and they have closed their eyes.

Otherwise they might see with their eyes,
hear with their ears,
understand with their hearts and turn,

and I would heal them."

By the time Jesus made His triumphal entry into Jerusalem during Passover week, the excitement and confusion—and hatred—surrounding Him had reached a fever pitch. The crowds lining the streets that day expected the imminent inauguration of an earthly kingdom to fulfill the words of Isaiah 9:7: "He will reign on David's throne and over his kingdom, establishing and upholding it with justice and righteousness from that time on and forever." Little did they know that Jesus' kingdom was not of this world.

Meanwhile, in the shadows, the religious leaders devised a wicked plot to destroy Him. They found a willing accomplice in Judas Iscariot, Jesus' traitorous disciple who agreed to betray the Lord for thirty pieces of silver—the meager price of a slave's life in the Old Testament.

As Thursday night of Passover bled into Friday morning, the leaders initiated their diabolical plan. Guided by Judas, an armed mob hunted down Jesus in the Garden of Gethsemane just outside Jerusalem, where He had been praying in anguish, knowing the terrible climax of His mission was at hand.

Jesus' arrest and the ensuing trials were a mockery. He had done nothing wrong. He deserved the mob's worship and allegiance, not their threats and violence. He was their Creator, yet He would soon willingly die because of their sins. They had no idea. They were spiritually blind. As they fettered Him, Jesus said, "This is your hour—when darkness reigns" (Luke 22:53).

Deserted by His disciples, Jesus was brought before a hastily gathered Sanhedrin, the Jewish high council, in the wee hours of the morning. The Sanhedrin produced false witnesses, who made bogus accusations against the Lord. As Matthew 26:59 says, "The chief priests and the whole Sanhedrin were looking for false evidence against Jesus so that they could put him to death."

After settling on a verdict of blasphemy, the Sanhedrin brought Jesus before Pontius Pilate, Palestine's Roman governor. Pilate had no interest in getting entangled in Jewish religious affairs. But the governor's weak will was no match for the malevolent resolve of the mob. Their vitriolic shouts echoed through the streets of Jerusalem:

> *Crucify him!* (Matthew 27:22)

Pilate demurred. He even brought out Barabbas, a murderous criminal, and placed him beside Jesus in a goodwill gesture, giving the crowd a choice of whom they wanted Pilate to release. All the while, Jesus remained silent, even when Pilate gave Him opportunities to defend Himself. As 1 Peter 2:23 says, "When they hurled their insults at him, he did not retaliate; when he suffered, he made no threats. Instead, he entrusted himself to him who judges justly." The mob chose Barabbas and amplified its rage toward the Sinless One:

> *Crucify him!* (Matthew 27:23)

Finally, Pilate caved in to their bloodlust. First, the soldiers scourged Jesus. Roman scourging was a horrifying form of torture where the victim was tied to a post and whipped repeatedly with leather straps containing fragments of bone and metal. It wasn't uncommon for the scourging to kill a prisoner before the final execution.

Next, Jesus was taken to the governor's fortress, where scores of soldiers encircled Him like a pack of wolves. Without mercy, they stripped Him to His undergarments, mocked Him, struck Him, spit in His face, and pressed a crown of thorns into His scalp, opening up deep, bloody wounds. Then they led away the Son of God to be crucified.

Crucifixion was one of the cruelest forms of death in history. Long spikes were driven through the victim's hands and feet and into a wooden cross, which was placed upright in the ground. The victim often suffered there for days, eventually succumbing to asphyxiation or the sheer physical trauma.

But crucifixions were more than just a means of capital punishment. The Romans also intended them to be humiliating public spectacles and frightening deterrents for future insubordination. Bodies often hung on crosses long after death, left to rot or be eaten by scavengers. Rome wanted to convey a brutally unmistakable message: break our laws and **this** will be your fate.

As for the Jews, they considered crucifixion victims to be under divine anathema, based on Deuteronomy 21:23: "You must not leave the body hanging on the pole overnight. Be sure to bury it that same day, because anyone who is hung on a pole is under God's curse."

For six hours, Jesus hung in agony upon the cross at Golgotha, an elevated mount nicknamed "The Skull" that was just outside Jerusalem's walls. Immediately below Him, Roman soldiers gambled for His clothing—the ultimate insult. The religious leaders and other passers-by jeered at Him. So did one of the two thieves hanging beside Him. Overhead, a supernatural veil of midday darkness—a visible manifestation of God's judgment on sin—blanketed Palestine.

Finally, after bearing the weight of humanity's sin, Jesus said, "It is finished" (John 19:30), and breathed His last. At that moment, according to Matthew 27:51–53, a huge earthquake shook the region, dead saints came back to life, and the massive curtain (measuring sixty feet high and thirty feet wide) that separated the Holy Place from the Most Holy Place in the temple was torn "from top to bottom"—all clearly divine acts. Jesus' death was a historically momentous event.

Slowly, the large crowds dispersed, awed and perhaps confused by what they had just witnessed. "But," Luke 23:49 says, "all those who knew him, including the women who had followed him from Galilee, stood at a distance, watching these things."

The disciples were flabbergasted. They had given up everything to follow Jesus. In Matthew 16:16, Peter had rightly confessed to Jesus, "You are the Messiah, the Son of the living God." But now Jesus was gone, His lifeless body hanging upon a cursed instrument of execution. Their hope, it seemed, was buried.

As the day ended, Joseph of Arimathea and Nicodemus the Pharisee, two secret followers of Jesus, took Jesus' body, wrapped it in linen cloths according to ancient Jewish burial customs, and placed it in a nearby garden tomb. Then they rolled a stone in front of the entrance. The following day, at the Jewish leaders' behest, Pilate ordered the tomb to be sealed and guarded in order to avoid any grave robbing.

Thus was fulfilled the words of Isaiah from some seven hundred years earlier:

> **He was despised and rejected by mankind,**
> **a man of suffering, and familiar with pain.**
> **Like one from whom people hide their faces**
> **he was despised, and we held him in low esteem.**
>
> **Surely he took up our pain**

and bore our suffering,
yet we considered him punished by God,
stricken by him, and afflicted.
But he was pierced for our transgressions,
he was crushed for our iniquities;
the punishment that brought us peace was on him,
and by his wounds we are healed.
We all, like sheep, have gone astray,
each of us has turned to our own way;
and the LORD has laid on him
the iniquity of us all.

He was oppressed and afflicted,
yet he did not open his mouth;
he was led like a lamb to the slaughter,
and as a sheep before its shearers is silent,
so he did not open his mouth.
By oppression and judgment he was taken away.
Yet who of his generation protested?

For he was cut off from the land of the living;
for the transgression of my people he was punished.
He was assigned a grave with the wicked,
and with the rich in his death,
though he had done no violence,
nor was any deceit in his mouth.

Yet it was the LORD's will to crush him and cause him to suffer,
and though the LORD makes his life an offering for sin,
he will see his offspring and prolong his days,
and the will of the LORD will prosper in his hand.
After he has suffered,
he will see the light of life and be satisfied;
by his knowledge my righteous servant will justify many,
and he will bear their iniquities.

Therefore I will give him a portion among
the great,
and he will divide the spoils with the
strong,
because he poured out his life unto death,
and was numbered with the transgressors.
For he bore the sin of many,
and made intercession for the transgres-
sors. (Isaiah 53:3–12)

CHAPTER 4

THE RESURRECTION

Jesus' death was tragic and unjust. But He was no martyr. He wasn't like William Wallace, Joan of Arc, Nathan Hale, or even the apostle Paul—dedicated individuals who died for a memorable cause.

No, Jesus' sacrifice was all part of God's redemptive plan. He wasn't forced into death. Beautifully, He allowed it. As He said in John 10:17–18, "The reason my Father loves me is that I lay down my life—only to take it up again. No one takes it from me, but I lay it down of my own accord. I have authority to lay it down and authority to take it up again."

This truth is also evidenced by the way Jesus died. Matthew 27:50 says, "And when Jesus had cried out again in a loud voice, he **gave up** his spirit" (emphasis added). Similarly, Luke 23:46 records that "Jesus called out with a loud voice, 'Father, into your hands I commit my spirit.' When he had said this, he breathed his last." Jesus, the eternal Son of God who created life itself (John 1:3), was fully in control of His death from start to finish.

As such, Jesus was fully in control of what happened next. In fact, the outcome had already been decided, as Acts 2:24 testifies, "because it was impossible for death to keep its hold on him."

Perhaps you're reading about Jesus' resurrection for the first time. Or maybe you've heard about it before but never given it much thought. If so, here's a word of encouragement: don't be like the people of Jesus' day who were "ever hearing but never understanding" (Mark 4:12). As you read on, allow the truth of Scripture to penetrate your soul—and then believe. Let the greatest moment in history—the hope of Easter—turn all questions, hesitations, and skepticism into life-transforming faith.

On the other hand, if you have already trusted in Christ, don't skim these pages. Never become too familiar with what 1 Peter 1:3–4 calls the "new birth into a living hope through the resurrection of Jesus Christ from the dead, and into an inheritance that can never perish, spoil or fade." Let Scripture's truth cause you to marvel and worship anew.

Early on the Sunday morning after Jesus died, a small group of women from Galilee entered a garden. The sun's rays were just beginning to illuminate the day. Most of Jerusalem and the surrounding villages were still asleep. It was a tranquil scene. But for these women, there was no serenity. Inside, they were a mishmash of chaotic emotions. Torrents of sorrow, confusion, and fear had flooded their minds for two full days. Their hearts felt like anchors. Bearing aromatic spices, they had come to the garden to anoint a dead man.

Then they stopped cold. The grave where the body had been laid several days earlier was open. The heavy stone at the entrance had been rolled away. They looked at each other, mouths agape in disbelief. Hurrying to the tomb, they peered inside and found it empty, except for linen burial cloths.

Suddenly, two men dressed in dazzling white appeared. Their blinding radiance sent the speechless women to their knees in fear and reverence. "Why do you look for the living among the dead?" the angels asked. "He is not here; he has risen!" (Luke 24:5–6).

He is risen? Is it really true? We saw His brutalized, lifeless body taken from the cross and interred. How can this be? . . . Wait, isn't this what He had told us before His death?

The women's minds raced, outpaced only by the beating of their hearts. One of them, Mary Magdalene, rushed to where the disciples were staying and reported the news. Peter and John, like two Olympic sprinters, raced to the grave. Both of them entered the tomb and saw the empty burial cloths, but no body. Then they returned home, scratching their heads.

When Mary Magdalene returned to the garden, the swirl of emotions inside her finally spilled over in tears. As she stood outside the tomb weeping, suddenly she noticed a man standing behind her. It was the Lord Jesus! He was really alive!

Shortly after, Jesus appeared to several of the other

women in the garden. Later that day, He appeared to two of His followers on the road to Emmaus and then to ten of His disciples in Jerusalem. Imagine their shock and excitement! Days earlier, they had personally witnessed His terrible death. Now, He was walking among them once more, displaying the nail scars in His hands and feet!

Jesus' resurrection is the greatest, most profound moment in history. It changed everything. You'd think that everyone who learned about this revolutionary event would react like Jesus' first-century followers did. But sadly, that's not the case.

The idea of the resurrection has always been a stumbling block for many. Over the centuries, there have been countless attempts to discredit its veracity. The attacks started mere hours after Jesus rose, when the Roman soldiers who fainted at the angels' appearance while guarding the tomb returned to the Jewish chief priests and told them what had happened. The priests quickly assembled an emergency meeting of the Sanhedrin. They decided to bribe the guards into spreading the lie that Jesus' disciples had stolen His body at night as they slept at their post.

Imagine that. Faced with irrefutable facts of Christ's resurrection, the religious leaders chose to spin a web of deceit rather than acknowledge the blatant truth and accept Jesus as their Lord and Savior. Their hearts were spiritually hardened. The same can still be said for anyone who denies Jesus' resurrection.

Today, the questions about the resurrection still linger. If you enter "Did the resurrection of Jesus really happen?" into an Internet search engine, you'll get hundreds of thousands of results. Clearly, it's still a question of significant interest and debate.

Nevertheless, the evidence supporting the resurrection's authenticity is overwhelming. Most of the twenty-seven New Testament letters, written by at least eight different authors over a span of about five decades, mention the risen Christ. What's more, Scripture records at least twelve distinct appearances of Jesus to His disciples and other believers following the resurrection:

- A group of women, including Mary Magdalene, Mary the mother of James, Salome, and Joanna, in the tomb garden on Resurrection

Sunday morning (Matthew 28:1–9; Mark 16:1; Luke 24:10), and possibly a separate appearance exclusive to Mary Magdalene (John 20:11–18)

- Peter on Sunday (Luke 24:34; 1 Corinthians 15:5)
- Two disciples (other than the Twelve) on the road to Emmaus on Sunday afternoon (Luke 24:13–32)
- A group of believers, including the eleven disciples but not Thomas, in Jerusalem on Sunday evening (Luke 24:33–49; John 20:19–25)
- The disciples, including Thomas, a week later (John 20:24–29)
- Seven disciples by the Sea of Galilee (John 21:1–23)
- The twelve disciples, including the newly appointed Matthias (Acts 1:23; 1 Corinthians 15:5)

- More than five hundred believers at once (1 Corinthians 15:6)
- James, Jesus' half brother (1 Corinthians 15:7)
- "All the apostles" (1 Corinthians 15:7)
- The eleven disciples on the Mount of Olives at His ascension (Matthew 28:16–17; Acts 1:6–11)
- Paul on the road to Damascus (Acts 9:1–9; 1 Corinthians 15:8)

The facts are there. But ultimately, it comes down to faith. Hebrews 11:1 defines **faith** as "confidence in what we hope for and assurance about what we do not see." And Hebrews 11:6 adds, "Without faith it is impossible to please God."

Jesus' resurrection happened two millennia ago in the Middle East, and many hundreds of people saw the risen Lord. But you didn't. Yet the Savior still calls you to believe. As Romans 10:9 says, "If you declare with your mouth, 'Jesus is Lord,' and believe in your heart that God raised him from the dead, you will be saved."

Do you believe in the historicity of the death, burial, and resurrection of Jesus Christ? More importantly, do you believe what these real events **mean**? Do you believe that Jesus' great sacrifice provides salvation from sins and eternal life to all who trust in Him?

If you doubt, there is still hope. Thomas, one of Jesus' disciples, struggled at first to accept the resurrection, according to John 20. He wasn't present with the others during Jesus' first appearance to His disciples on the evening of Resurrection Sunday. So when the disciples saw Thomas afterward, their excitement spilled out: "We have seen the Lord!" they exclaimed. But Thomas refused to believe. "Unless I see the nail marks in his hands and put my finger where the nails were, and put my hand into his side," he grumbled, "I will not believe" (John 20:25).

One week later, Jesus appeared again to His disciples, and Thomas was present. The Lord invited His friend to touch the scars of His sacrifice. Thomas was undone. "My Lord and my God!" he cried. Jesus replied, “Because you have seen me, you have believed; blessed are those who have not seen and yet have believed” (John 20:28–29).

That heavenly blessing—rich with hope and rewards—is a promise for you, if you believe. Though your eyes can’t see Jesus now, have you believed? Have you proclaimed Him as your Lord and your God? Does your hope rest in the risen Savior?

CHAPTER 5

WHAT THE RESURRECTION ACCOMPLISHED

If the hope of Easter is found in Jesus' resurrection, the logical question that follows is this: What did the resurrection actually accomplish? In other words, what hope does it provide? Why does a miracle that happened two thousand years ago in ancient Palestine matter today?

The resurrection matters in every way! Its spiritual and eternal import can't be overstated. It was the culmination of the divine salvation plan, ensuring the fulfillment of every redemptive purpose the Father, Son, and Holy Spirit had prepared in eternity past.

The resurrection guarantees life-changing hope to all who believe, both in this life and the life to come. Out of the resurrection flow many truths about Jesus Himself, as well as practical, everyday blessings for all believers and marvelous eternal promises.

First, let's look at four truths about Jesus that His resurrection reveals:

The Resurrection Validated All of Jesus' Claims About Himself

One day as Jesus was walking among the temple grounds, the Jewish religious leaders confronted Him and asked Him point-blank, "If you are the Messiah, tell us plainly" (John 10:24). Jesus admonished them for their hard-heartedness, turned the conversation toward His relationship with God the Father, and then declared, "I and the Father are one" (John 10:30).

It was a staggering statement—enough that Jesus' opponents tried to stone Him for blasphemy. But it was only one of many such declarations that Jesus made during His time on earth. He also claimed to be sinless (John 8:29), eternal (John 10:28), "the resurrection and the life" (John 11:25), and to possess the authority to forgive sins (Luke 5:20). What's more, Jesus (correctly) predicted His own death and resurrection many times (John 10:17; 16:16; Luke 18:33). These were all clear claims to deity, for who can back up all these audacious statements except God alone? Had

Jesus remained in the grave, He would've been reduced to history's greatest fraud. Instead, the resurrection proved that all of Jesus' claims were true. After all, no one has the power over death except the One who created life.

By virtue of the resurrection, Jesus proved that He is the eternal Son of God who has the power over life and death and is worthy of all our faith and worship. This gives us present hope because we know we have a Savior who is fully trustworthy! He really is "the way and the truth and the life," as He proclaimed in John 14:6. All who are weary and burdened can find rest in Him, as He promised in Matthew 11:28. Our faith in Him will be greatly rewarded!

The Resurrection Proved That Jesus Is the Only Way to Heaven

There are countless religions in the world, and lots of people believe that many roads lead to heaven. Others cynically ask, "How can you be so sure that Christianity is right and all other belief systems are wrong?"

The resurrection provides the answer. No other

religious figure in history claimed to be God and then backed it up by conquering death. As such, Jesus' words in John 14:6 are perfectly and powerfully true: "I am the way and the truth and the life. No one comes to the Father except through me." Acts 4:12 also bears this out: "Salvation is found in no one else, for there is no other name under heaven given to mankind by which we must be saved." In a world saturated with many belief systems, the resurrection provides rock-solid assurance that Christianity is the only true faith and Jesus is the only true Savior.

The Resurrection Validated Jesus as Head of the Church

In Matthew 16, Acts 1, and elsewhere in Scripture, Jesus foretold the advent of the church. Acts 2 describes the fulfillment of His prophecy on the Day of Pentecost—about fifty days after His resurrection—when the Holy Spirit descended upon a group of believers in Jerusalem in miraculous power, sparking the genesis and rapid spread of Christianity.

The church is the collective, worldwide body of Jesus' true followers that represents Him on earth following His ascension into heaven. Its mission is to reflect God's glory (1 Corinthians 10:31) through various Spirit-endowed gifts (1 Corinthians 12) and proclaim the gospel of salvation through Jesus to all nations (Matthew 28:19–20).

At the head of the church is Christ Himself. Just as a dead king can't rule a country and a dead CEO can't oversee a corporation, a dead savior could never lead the church. But Jesus isn't dead! Colossians 1:18 affirms, "And he is the head of the body, the church; he is the beginning and the firstborn from among the dead, so that in everything he might have the supremacy." The risen Lord's complete, loving authority over His church gives us present hope in all we do as a body of believers.

The Resurrection Positioned Jesus as Our Great High Priest

In the Old Testament, the Jewish high priest performed many important functions as Israel's spiritual leader. None, though, was more important than his role on the Day of Atonement, the one day of the year when he—and only he—was allowed to pass through the curtain and enter the temple's Most Holy Place to make a sacrifice for the sins of the people (Leviticus 16). In this way, the ritually cleansed priest interceded and atoned for the morally flawed nation.

In vivid detail, Hebrews 4–10 shows how Christ is the ultimate fulfillment of the Old Testament Law and its elaborate sacrificial and priestly system, ushering in the new covenant of hope and redemption through His blood. This was only possible because Jesus is "a great high priest who has passed through the heavens" (Hebrews 4:14, ESV), an allusion to His death, resurrection, and ascension. Romans 8:34 clarifies the connection between Jesus' resurrection and perfect priesthood when it says, "Christ Jesus who died—more than that, who was raised to life—is at the right hand of God and is also interceding for us." What great hope we have in the fact that our Savior is also our great High Priest, perfectly representing us before the Father!

* * *

While the resurrection reveals wonderful truths about Christ, it also showers believers with immediate hope in this life. Here are seven examples:

The Resurrection Validated Jesus' Atoning Work on the Cross

Death is both the punishment for sin (Romans 6:23) and God's compulsory payment for the forgiveness of sins (Hebrews 9:22). His holiness and justice require this. He was perfectly within His rights to pour out His wrath and completely destroy sinful mankind. Yet in His mercy, He instituted a sacrificial system for Old Testament Israel where priests would slaughter spotless lambs and other animals to temporarily atone, or make payment, for the sins of the people.

When Jesus came, He provided once-for-all atonement for sins as the true Lamb of God (Hebrews 7:27). Jesus perfectly became our "propitiation" (Romans 3:25 ESV)—a wrath-bearing sacrifice. But a sacrificial death alone was not enough to save us. A dead savior is really no savior at all, just as the blood of livestock was only a provisional solution (Hebrews 10:4). Jesus' resurrection proved that God had fully accepted His death as the everlasting redemption payment for our sins. As Romans 1:4 says, Jesus "was appointed [or confirmed as] the Son of God in power by his resurrection."

Today, if you've repented and trusted in Jesus, you can rest assured that your sins have been completely atoned for. Your salvation isn't up for debate. God is completely satisfied with His Son's sacrifice, and you are the beneficiary of this great exchange!

The Resurrection Guarantees Believers' Regeneration

Every human starts out in serious trouble. As discussed in chapter 2, we are all sinful in nature (Romans 5:19) and deed (Romans 3:23). We all need a new spiritual birth—a new, regenerated heart that is cleansed from sin's guilt. This is what Jesus was referring to in John 3:3 when He said, "No one can see the kingdom of God unless they are born again." Left to ourselves, this spiritual transformation is impossible since we all started life "dead in [our] transgressions and sins" (Ephesians 2:1). A dead man can't change his condition. After all, he's **dead**!

But there's hope! Through a wonderful, mysterious work of the Spirit, God regenerates spiritually dead hearts to make them alive in Christ. In other words, He mercifully awakens sinful hearts to receive the gospel in faith. First Peter 1:3 clearly testifies that this miraculous heart change, described as "new birth," is only possible through the empty tomb: "Praise be to the God and Father of our Lord Jesus Christ! In his great mercy he has given us new birth into a living hope through the resurrection of Jesus Christ from the dead."

The Resurrection Guarantees Believers' Justification

Justification is a theological term that simply means "to be made right with God." It's a legal declaration where God responds to our saving faith in Christ's atoning work (that He imparts to us through Spirit-empowered regeneration) by declaring us completely forgiven and righteous (guiltless) before Him.

Scripture says that God imputed, or credited, every believer's sin-guilt to Jesus on the cross (1 Peter 2:24) while imputing Jesus' righteousness to us (Romans 5:19). It's the deal of a lifetime! Romans 4:25 clearly speaks to the resurrection's necessity in this incredible transaction: "He was delivered over to death for our sins and was raised to life for our justification."

Once you are justified before God, it's a done deal. Jesus' death and resurrection were enough to purchase your complete forgiveness. There's nothing more for you to add. You can't earn God's favor; Christ purchased it for you. If you're carrying any guilt or shame, you can lay it down before the cross. Through faith in Christ, your sins have been fully covered—forever!

The Resurrection Fills Every Christian with Heavenly Power

As a kid, did you ever covet Superman's ability to fly, Spider-Man's web-slinging skills, or Wonder Woman's regenerative abilities? Through Christ, you have far greater power at your disposal.

Amazingly, the same otherworldly power that raised Jesus from the dead and lifted Him into heaven is available to all believers. As Paul wrote in Ephesians 1:18–20,

> *I pray that the eyes of your heart may be enlightened in order that you may know the hope to which he has called*

you, the riches of his glorious inheritance in his holy people, and his incomparably great power for us who believe. That power is the same as the mighty strength he exerted when he raised Christ from the dead and seated him at his right hand in the heavenly realms.

The next time you're feeling physically or spiritually weak, remember that, in Christ, the same divine power that predestines, calls, regenerates, justifies, sanctifies, and ultimately glorifies sinners now lives inside of you! Are you struggling with depression? Are personal trials overwhelming you? Are you fighting a persistent sin pattern? Are you suffering persecution for your faith? If you are in Christ, there is resurrection power inside you to help!

The Resurrection Makes Sanctification Possible

Improvement is a good thing. As humans, we want to improve in our studies, jobs, athletic abilities, relationships, parenting, and other areas. Spiritually speaking, the same should be true. Christians should never settle for status quo. Thanks to Jesus' resurrection, the gradual improvement process of sanctification is guaranteed to all believers.

Sanctification is the lifelong progression where a Christian steadily becomes less sinful and more like Christ through the Holy Spirit's power. Colossians 3:1–4 alludes to the resurrection's part in this:

> *Since, then, you have been raised with Christ, set your hearts on things above, where Christ is, seated at the right hand of God. Set your minds on things above, not on earthly things. For you died, and your life is now hidden with Christ in God. When Christ, who is your life, appears, then you also will appear with him in glory.*

Day by day, Christians become more like their Savior to reflect His glory!

The Resurrection Empowers Fruitfulness in God's Kingdom

While Jesus was on earth, He prophesied about the Holy Spirit's new indwelling of believers after the resurrection and ascension. In fact, Jesus said it was **better** for Him to leave and make way for the Spirit's arrival (John 16:7).

Why? Because the Spirit would bring new conviction about sin (John 16:8), inhabit believers to make them God's new dwelling place (1 Corinthians 3:16), and empower them to do good works, build one another up, and spread the gospel. As Acts 1:8 says, "But you will receive power when the Holy Spirit comes on you; and you will be my witnesses in Jerusalem, and in all Judea and Samaria, and to the ends of the earth." Through the risen Savior, God gives believers a spiritual mission and then empowers them to accomplish it by His Spirit's power!

The Resurrection Seals Our Eternal Security as Believers

Salvation is not based on human accomplishments but by divine sovereignty and power (Ephesians 1:3–14). It is completely a work of God's grace (Ephesians 2:8–9) through the all-sufficient death and resurrection of our Savior.

Paul affirmed this doctrine and connected it to the resurrection when he wrote Romans 8:34–39:

> *Who then is the one who condemns? No one. Christ Jesus who died—more than that, who was raised to life—is at the right hand of God and is also interceding for us. Who shall separate us from the love of Christ? Shall trouble or hardship or persecution or famine or nakedness or danger or sword? As it is written:*
>
> *"For your sake we face death all day long; we are considered as sheep to be slaughtered."*

No, in all these things we are more than conquerors through him who loved us. For I am convinced that neither death nor life, neither angels nor demons, neither the present nor the future, nor any powers, neither height nor depth, nor anything else in all creation, will be able to separate us from the love of God that is in Christ Jesus our Lord.

What a blessing to know that when God saves us, He does so powerfully and completely, without the possibility of failure, all through the finished work of His Son!

* * *

Do you see how Jesus' resurrection gives present hope to all who believe? Because Christ is alive and reigning over all creation, the spiritual benefits that we can experience right now are stunning. But that's not all. The risen Savior also provides incredible hope for the life to come. Here are three ways:

The Resurrection Assures Believers of Ultimate Victory over Evil

Imagine if the Allied forces invading the Normandy beaches during World War II had been guaranteed that they'd win in the end. What a difference that would've made in the soldiers' lives!

Christians have an even better guarantee. In this life, believers are locked in a heated battle with the forces of evil (Ephesians 6:12). But thanks to Jesus, the outcome has already been determined. As Acts 17:31 says, "For he [God] has set a day when he will judge the world with justice by the man he has appointed. He has given proof of this to everyone by raising him from the dead."

The resurrection provides fail-proof confidence of eternal victory to every believer. When Jesus died and rose again, He landed a fatal blow to Satan, sin, and all evil. As Colossians 2:15 says, "And having disarmed the powers and authorities, he made a public spectacle of them, triumphing over them by the cross." First John 3:8 gets more specific: "The reason the Son of God appeared was to destroy the devil's work." And Revelation 20:10 describes Satan's ultimate doom: "And the devil, who deceived them, was thrown into the lake of burning sulfur, where the beast and the false prophet had been thrown. They will be tormented day and night for ever and ever." Revelation 21 then talks about the perfection of the new heaven and new earth, where evil is absent and righteousness reigns.

Christians get to savor the Savior's all-encompassing victory, both now and in the life to come. "But thanks be to God!" Paul wrote in 1 Corinthians 15:57. "He gives us the victory through our Lord Jesus Christ."

The Resurrection Guarantees Eternal Life to All Believers

Benjamin Franklin once said, "In this world, nothing can be said to be certain, except death and taxes." For every Christian, though, physical death will always be followed by spiritual (and eventually bodily) immortality in the presence of our Savior, thanks to the resurrection.

The risen Lord became the "firstfruits," or forerunner, of our own resurrection (1 Corinthians 15:20). In Romans 8:10–11, Paul wrote, "But if Christ is in you, then even though your body is subject to death because of sin, the Spirit gives life because of righteousness. And if the Spirit of him who raised Jesus from the dead is living in you, he who raised Christ from the dead will also give life to your mortal bodies because of his Spirit who lives in you."

Jesus Himself promised eternal life to all believers many times, including in John 11:25 when He spoke these well-known words: "I am the resurrection and the life. The one who believes in me will live, even though they die." This is all possible because Christ destroyed the power of death. In fact, Revelation 20:14 says that death will one day be thrown into the lake of fire.

In eternity, believers will be clothed, just like their Savior, with new resurrection bodies that will never deteriorate or die. As 1 Corinthians 15:53–54 says, "For the perishable must clothe itself with the imperishable, and the mortal with immortality. When the perishable has been clothed with the imperishable, and the mortal with immortality, then the saying that is written will come true: 'Death has been swallowed up in victory.'" What a glorious promise!

The Resurrection Foreshadows Jesus' Second Coming

As the disciples were standing, mouths agape, on the Mount of Olives following Jesus' ascension, two angels visited them with a wonderful message. 'Men of Galilee,' they said, 'why do you stand here looking into the sky? This same Jesus, who has been taken from you into heaven, will come back in the same way you have seen him go into heaven' (Acts 1:11).

Two thousand years later, we are still waiting for this glorious promise to be fulfilled. But we wait with hope—excitedly expecting a guaranteed outcome. One day, the risen Lord will return to earth in overwhelming power and majesty (2 Thessalonians 1:7) to redeem His people (1 Thessalonians 4:13–18), vanquish all evil (Malachi 4:1), and inaugurate His eternal kingdom (Revelation 11:15) where we will enjoy His beautiful presence forever

(1 Thessalonians 4:17). This is the future hope for all believers and should motivate us to live in a way worthy of our heavenly calling as we await the return of our Savior (2 Peter 3:11–14).

* * *

This is by no means an exhaustive list. We will never fully mine the depths of the resurrection's spiritual riches.

Still, are you beginning to see the hope that we have in the risen Lord Jesus Christ? Are you starting to comprehend the glories of the salvation He freely offers? Jesus' love is a bottomless fountain that never stops flowing for all who trust in Him.

CHAPTER 6

REIGNING ON HIGH

"The right hand of God."

It's one of the most powerful phrases in Scripture. Throughout the Bible, this symbolic expression is used to describe divine strength, majesty, and authority. In Exodus 15:6, Moses extolled the Almighty's right hand in song after Israel's deliverance from Egypt: "Your right hand, LORD, was majestic in power. Your right hand, LORD, shattered the enemy." Likewise, Psalm 48:10 says that God's "right hand is filled with righteousness," and Isaiah 41:10 describes how the Lord promises to "uphold you with my righteous right hand."

God's right hand is also a position of supreme honor and glory, reserved for only the most privileged individuals. In Psalm 16, King David wrote, "You make known to me the path of life; you will fill me with joy in your presence, with eternal pleasures at your right hand" (verse 11). This is where the risen Lord Jesus Christ is now seated.

The apostle Peter proclaimed this to the multitude in Jerusalem during his Day of Pentecost sermon: "God has raised this Jesus to life, and . . . exalted [Him] to the right hand of God" (Acts 2:32–33). Stephen, the first Christian martyr, saw Christ there just before he was stoned to death. "'Look,' he said, 'I see heaven open and the Son of Man standing at the right hand of God'" (Acts 7:56). Jesus Himself predicted this before His death: "But from now on," He told the Sanhedrin during His trial, "the Son of Man will be seated at the right hand of the mighty God" (Luke 22:69).

Jesus has occupied this position of ultimate honor and supremacy for the two thousand years since His ascension. He reigns over all creation, holding the entire universe together (Colossians 1:17) and "sustaining all things by his powerful word" (Hebrews 1:3).

But Christ's exaltation doesn't equate to inapproachability. He is intimately involved in the life of every believer. As our perfect High Priest, He intercedes for us (Romans 8:34), empathizes with our weaknesses (Hebrews 4:15), and helps strengthen our faith (Hebrews 4:14). He is present among believers when they pray together (Matthew 18:20). He actively guides His church (Ephesians 1:22) and sanctifies it (Revelation 2–3). Even His last words on earth, in Matthew 28:20, were wonderfully personal: "And surely I am with you always, to the very end of the age."

That's not all, though. Currently, Jesus is preparing an eternal home for all true believers (John 14:2) and awaiting the God-ordained day when He will return to earth a final time to eradicate evil (Hebrews 10:12–13) and redeem His people forever (1 Thessalonians 4:16–17).

In the new heaven and new earth, saints will eternally enjoy God's renewed creation, which will be restored to its original state of paradise forever. (Think of the delights found on the most exotic Polynesian island and multiple them by, oh, a billion or so.)

In heaven, there will be no sin. No sadness. No suffering. No death. Revelation 22:3 says, "No longer will there be any curse. The throne of God and of the Lamb will be in the city, and his servants will serve him."

Best yet, believers will get to eternally bask in the glory of the Lord and fellowship with Christ like never before. "God's dwelling place is now among the people, and he will dwell with them," Revelation 21:3 promises. "They will be his people, and God himself will be with them and be their God." And Revelation 22:3–4 says, "The throne of God and of the Lamb will be in the city, and his servants will serve him. They will see his face, and his name will be on their foreheads." Those are some of the most beautiful words in Scripture. The redeemed will see Jesus face to face!

But what, exactly, will believers see when they look upon their Savior? During His life on earth, Jesus' appearance was nondescript: "He had no beauty or majesty to attract us to him, nothing in his appearance that we should desire him," according to Isaiah 53:2. In death, His appearance was "disfigured beyond that of any human being and his form marred beyond human likeness" (Isaiah 52:14).

Not anymore. The risen and glorified Son of God is luminously magnificent beyond human description. While the full details of Jesus' appearance remain a mystery, Scripture provides some fascinating hints at His indescribable radiance and majesty.

Peter, James, and John got a sneak peek during the Transfiguration. Matthew 17:2 explains Jesus' glorified appearance this way: "His face shone like the sun, and his clothes became as white as the light."

Paul experienced something similar during his life-changing encounter with the risen Lord on the Damascus Road. Paul (then called Saul) was traveling around noon as the sun was near its zenith. It was a bright, hot day. Yet we read in Acts that "a light from heaven" flashed around him, dwarfing the sun's brightness (Acts 26:13). In fact, the Greek word for **blazing** is the same word used in ancient times to describe a lightning bolt's brilliance. Christ's post-resurrection glory was so powerful, it knocked Paul to the ground and blinded him for three days.

Roughly sixty years later, just before the turn of the second century, John experienced Scripture's greatest recorded vision of the risen Lord's unrestrained glory during his apocalyptic visions on the island of Patmos. In Revelation 1:13–16, he wrote,

> *And among the lampstands was someone like a son of man, dressed in a robe reaching down to his feet and with a golden sash around his chest. The hair on his head was white like wool, as white as snow, and his eyes were like blazing fire. His feet were like bronze glowing in a furnace, and his voice was like the sound of rushing waters. In his right hand he held seven stars, and coming out of his mouth was a sharp, double-edged sword. His face was like the sun shining in all its brilliance.*

It's clear that John was at a loss for words, grasping for the best earthly metaphors he could think of—wool, snow, fire, hot metal, turbulent waters, military weapons—to describe the glorified Son of God. When John witnessed this astounding sight, he "fell at his feet as though dead" (Revelation 1:17).

This is the resurrected Lord Jesus Christ. This awesome, loving, yet fearful Ruler—reigning over the entire universe at God the Father's right hand—is the hope of Easter.

CHAPTER 7

WORSHIP AND AWE

Whenever anyone encountered the resurrected Savior in the New Testament, their reaction was always the same. They fell at His feet in worship and awe—always in spirit, but often literally as well:

- The women who witnessed the empty tomb "clasped his feet and worshiped him." (Matthew 28:9)
- When the disciples saw Him the evening of Resurrection Sunday, they were "overjoyed." (John 20:20)
- Peter once jumped out of a boat and swam a hundred yards when he saw Jesus on the shore. (John 21)
- After seeing Jesus on the Damascus Road, Paul "fell to the ground." (Acts 9:4)
- In Revelation 5:8, the heavenly throng "fell down before the Lamb" and sang a song of praise

Is that your posture this Easter season? Are you falling at Jesus' feet in wonder and adoration? Regardless of how many times you've considered the resurrection, your heart's position should mirror that of Jesus' disciples on that first Easter Sunday: Worship the Savior. Love Him. Embrace Him. Kneel before Him—for the first time or the five hundredth—and declare that He is Lord.

The resurrection is the proof: Jesus is the eternal Son of God, the one who fulfilled God's plan of salvation from ages past. He is the Messiah, the one whose arrival the prophets foretold long before that extraordinary night in Bethlehem. He is the sacrificial Lamb, offering up Himself as the payment for our sins. He is the King of kings and Lord of lords, the one who conquered death, sin, and Satan through His finished work on the cross. As the prophet Isaiah foretold centuries before Christ's incarnation, "In his name the nations will put their hope" (Matthew 12:21).

There's that word again: **hope**—"the eager expectation of a guaranteed outcome." For everyone who trusts in Jesus as their Lord and Savior, He is their certain hope for justification before God. He is their hope for heavenly adoption. He is their hope for eternal life.

Have you not yet believed? Don't wait another day! As 2 Corinthians 6:2 says, "I tell you, now is the time of God's favor, now is the day of salvation." This salvation cannot be earned; it is a free gift of God's grace. But it must be received. There's no magical formula—no specific prayer you have to recite. It's simply a matter of repentance (turning from sin) and faith (trusting in Christ's finished, redemptive work on your behalf). John 3:16 explains: "For God so loved the world that he gave his one and only Son, that whoever believes in him shall not perish but have eternal life."

Have you already believed? Then let the Holy Spirit stir your passions anew to follow Christ, conforming to His glorious image and forsaking all else. Pray for God's kingdom to come and His will to be done in your life. Continue to trust in the One who gave His life for yours, heeding the words of Hebrews 10:23: "Let us hold unswervingly to the hope we profess, for he who promised is faithful."

Christian, praise the Lord for the hope in Christ that is your current reality: a regenerated heart, forgiveness, redemption, the Spirit's indwelling, and much more. Exalt also in the hope of blessings to come: continued sanctification, Jesus' return, freedom from sin's curse, a glorified body, and eternal life. This hope calls for endurance. As Romans 8:25 says, "But if we hope for what we do not yet have, we wait for it patiently."

Yes, **hope** is a beautiful word. Deep down, it's what each of us longs for—something to look forward to, something to believe in, something to live for. True hope is found only in the Son of God, who died in your place and rose again.

The Lord Jesus Christ is the hope of Easter. He is the hope of salvation. He is the hope of life everlasting. Put your hope in Him!